Text by Bob Ferrante and Tim Linafelt
Photos by Ross Obley

Head coach Jimbo Fisher celebrates with his team as Florida State was presented the Coaches' Trophy after defeating Auburn 34–31 in the BCS National Championship Game.

This book is book is available in quantity at special discounts for your group or organization. For further information, contact:

Triumph Books LLC
814 North Franklin Street
Chicago, Illinois 60610
Phone: (312) 337-0747
www.triumphbooks.com

Printed in U.S.A.
ISBN: 978-1-60078-894-9

Content packaged by Mojo Media, Inc.
Joe Funk: Editor
Jason Hinman: Creative Director

All interior photos by Ross Obley unless otherwise indicated.

Front cover photo by USA TODAY Sports Images
Back cover photo by Ross Obley

CONTENTS

BACK ON TOP

FLORIDA STATE RELOADS TO ENJOY DOMINANT 2013 SEASON

The Florida State Seminoles entered Jimbo Fisher's fourth season at the helm facing as many questions as ever since Fisher took over as head coach in 2010.

Questions about how they would replace the 11 players from last year's 12–2 ACC Championship team who were selected in the NFL Draft.

Questions about how Fisher would cope with the loss of seven of his assistant coaches—six from the year before and one who bolted after only a month on the job.

And a big question about exactly who would be making his first start under center when the Seminoles began their season at Pittsburgh.

Those questions and several others added up to the idea that these Seminoles shouldn't be this good. Not this fast. Not this year.

A national championship might be on the horizon, but first the team would have to go through some growing pains.

It turns out, though, that Fisher and the Seminoles made all the right moves, had all the right answers.

And it all culminated on January 6 in Pasadena, California, where, in their first appearance at the famed Rose Bowl Stadium, the Seminoles topped Auburn, 34–31, to claim their third football national championship and first since 1999.

"This is what you play for, this is what you prepare for," Fisher said. "Like I always talk about, a team has a one-year identity, a one-year life span, and that is the ultimate goal."

FSU began the season with a fairly anonymous No. 11 national ranking. But it didn't take long for the Seminoles to announce themselves as major players for that ultimate goal.

After winning a months-long quarterback competition that position coach Randy Sanders still insists was "not a unanimous thing," Jameis Winston, a redshirt freshman from Hueytown, Alabama, led the Seminoles to Pittsburgh's Heinz Field for a primetime, Labor Day contest that marked the Panthers' inaugural game as members of the Atlantic Coast Conference.

What followed was one of the most remarkable freshman debuts in modern college football history.

Winston's night began with a 13-yard completion to sophomore receiver Kelvin Benjamin. And then a 20-yard hookup with senior Kenny Shaw.

In the end, all came up roses for Florida State in the BCS National Championship Game at the Rose Bowl in Pasadena, California. Seminoles head coach Jimbo Fisher kissed the Coaches' Trophy during the presentation after the game.

And then nine more completed passes before he finally made a mark in the "incomplete" column. And even that was a pass that Shaw caught just barely out of bounds.

By the time the clock hit zero, Winston had completed 25-of-27 passes (92.5 percent) for 356 yards and four touchdowns, and the Seminoles routed Pittsburgh 41–13.

From there, Florida State's avalanche continued to roll.

As weeks passed, the Seminoles posted rout after rout, pausing only for a brief, first-half scare on September 28 at Boston College. Even then, FSU erased an early 14-point deficit by halftime and came away with a 48–34 victory, its closest of the season.

"That was a critical [moment]. I loved the way we handled it," Fisher said. "We were down 17–3, and our guys never blinked, came right back."

Otherwise, the Seminoles were never seriously threatened, and that includes a midseason showdown at then-No. 3 Clemson, where Winston became a household name by telling his teammates to "put a smile" on their faces during a televised pregame speech. He then went out and threw for 444 yards and three touchdowns in a 51–14 romp that propelled FSU to No. 2 in the BCS standings.

By the time the Seminoles completed their 45–7 pasting of Duke at the ACC Championship Game, they had outscored their opponents by a combined 689–139 and entered the BCS National Championship Game just 28 points away from becoming the highest scoring team in college football history.

And they had ascended to their first No. 1 national ranking since 2000.

"The NCAA has all these rules," Winston said. "But it does not say you cannot blow out everybody you play. That's the mentality we took."

Winston and the offense, of course, didn't do it all by themselves.

They were aided by a remarkable season from the FSU defense, which in its first season under coordinator Jeremy Pruitt posted No. 1 national rankings in passing yards allowed (152.0), passing efficiency defense (90.90), passing yards allowed per completion (4.94), and passes intercepted (25).

FSU's defenders scored eight touchdowns this season and, because of the lopsided nature of most games, the Seminoles' first-team defense spent most second halves watching from the sidelines.

Florida State's first-stringers entered the BCS National Championship Game having not allowed a single rushing touchdown.

"Our motto on the defense is: it's on us," senior linebacker Telvin Smith said. "In order to be a great team you have to have a great defense, no matter if the offensive is okay, mediocre or whatever, you've got to have a great and solid defense."

As the wins mounted, so, too, did the accolades.

Winston won the school's third Heisman Trophy, joining Charlie Ward (1993) and Chris Weinke (2000) as FSU's recipients of college football's highest individual honor. And he also took home the Walter Camp and Davey O'Brien Awards, among a slew of others.

He wasn't the only one. Bryan Stork, a fifth-year

P.J. Williams, Terrence Brooks, and Kelvin Benjamin celebrate with Florida State's national championship sign on the field at the Rose Bowl following FSU's win over Auburn.

senior, earned the Rimington Trophy as the nation's top center. Kicker Roberto Aguayo earned the Lou Groza Award. And defensive back Lamarcus Joyner and tight end Nick O'Leary were each finalists for their positions' highest honors.

All told, the Seminoles featured one unanimous All-American (Joyner), two consensus All-Americans (Joyner and Winston), 10 All-America selections, and 17 All-ACC selections.

Joyner, a South Florida native who was one of the signature recruits of Fisher's first signing class, raised some eyebrows by returning for his senior season rather than trying his hand in the NFL.

He maintained for months that he returned to finish what he started—to win a national title at FSU.

That he and his teammates did it comes as no surprise to him.

"I have faith and belief in the players and the coaches here," Joyner said. "I expected things like this to happen for us. Now, could I have told the country that? No, I couldn't have. But I understood the direction we were heading in. And these are the things we expected."

For more than a decade following Florida State's run of dominance in the 1990s, the Seminoles' football program has been dogged by a question, asked often as it tried to climb out of a stretch of prolonged mediocrity in the 2000s.

Are the Seminoles back? And when, if ever, will they be?

The road has been long and not always smooth, but on a cool Monday night in Pasadena, that road reached its end. The Seminoles are indeed back. Back on top of the college football world. ■

True freshman Kermit Whitfield celebrates with Florida State fans at the Rose Bowl following the Seminoles' win. Whitfield's kickoff return for a touchdown in the fourth quarter was a key play in the victory.

BCS NATIONAL CHAMPIONSHIP GAME

Florida State 34, Auburn 31
January 6, 2014 · Pasadena, California

AN INSTANT CLASSIC

WITH JUST 13 SECONDS REMAINING, TD SEALS FSU'S THIRD NATIONAL CHAMPIONSHIP

In a season of dominating performances, Florida State was bound to have a nail-biter.

If there was one question about FSU's résumé, the knock on an otherwise stellar and dominating season, it was that the Seminoles hadn't faced a situation where their backs were against the wall.

FSU had indeed rallied from a 17–3 deficit at Boston College to take a 48–34 victory. And pulled away after leading Miami at the half 21–14 to win 41–14.

But what if the Seminoles were trailing in the fourth quarter? How would FSU react—and could they come back? And could they do it against an SEC team?

The critics were wrong to doubt. FSU needed not one but two comebacks for the program's third national title.

Freshman quarterback Jameis Winston, fighting through his worst night during a Heisman Trophy season, was staring down two major problems: Auburn's defense was protecting 80 yards of green grass, and there was just 1 minute and 12 seconds on the clock.

So Winston, who was celebrating his 20th birthday, took charge in a moment that will live on in championship game history. In a stadium that has hosted 100 Rose Bowls and plenty of Super Bowls, Winston provided late-game drama that was up there with some of the finest performances of all-time in the stadium.

"I wanted to be in that situation because that's what great quarterbacks do," Winston said. "That's what the Tom Bradys, Peyton Mannings, Drew Brees, that's what they do."

Winston began to complete passes like he had done all season. He was 6-of-7 on the drive, including a 49-yard catch-and-run by Rashad Greene that set up FSU at the Auburn 23.

And with 13 seconds left, after a seesaw five minutes to wrap up the final BCS championship game, Winston found Kelvin Benjamin in the end zone for a 2-yard touchdown reception that gave Florida State a 34–31 victory at the Rose Bowl.

Jameis Winston cemented his place in college football history against Auburn in the BCS National Championship Game. The Heisman Trophy winner led Florida State 80 yards down the field for the winning touchdown in the game's final minute.

Jimbo Fisher won his first national title in January 2004 as LSU's offensive coordinator. On Monday night, he won a title in his fourth season as FSU's head coach.

Fisher's predecessor, coaching legend Bobby Bowden, was on the sideline as an honorary captain on Monday. Bowden won national titles with FSU in 1993 and '99, and he always said one of his hopes was to play in a Rose Bowl.

It never came true, but on Monday, Bowden was able to watch the program that he built win a title.

This was all part of Fisher's plan when he took over from Bowden in 2010. Fisher felt that FSU could be playing for a national title in 4 to 5 years.

He built one impressive signing class after another and created a team that is No. 1 in 2013. But he also rebuilt a program. FSU is most certainly back.

"It's been a four-year evolution to put ourselves in this opportunity," Fisher said. "We talked about being a program and we wanted to do things right and we wanted to build the foundation. These guys have given their hearts and souls to us as coaches, and it's been unbelievable."

And FSU needed every minute to pull out the victory.

The Seminoles rallied from an 18-point deficit, going ahead 27–24 with 4:31 to go on Kermit Whitfield's 100-yard kickoff return for a touchdown.

The Seminoles appeared to have completed the rally.

Auburn answered, using a 37-yard touchdown by Tre Mason to go up 31–27 with 1:19 to go. Mason had 195 of Auburn's 232 rushing yards.

The Tigers appeared to have pulled off yet another miracle.

But then Winston put together a seven-play, 80-yard touchdown drive in just 58 seconds. On first-and-goal from the 2, he found Benjamin

Running back Devonta Freeman powers downfield during Florida State's game-winning drive. The junior from Miami gained 73 yards on 11 carries to lead all FSU rushers.

Defensive back P.J. Williams brings down Auburn's Sammie Coates. The Florida State defense stepped up their game in the second half, holding Auburn scoreless in the third quarter and limiting the Tigers to a touchdown and field goal in the fourth as FSU came back from an 11-point halftime deficit.

"It's the fourth quarter, I've got one or two touches left and you can take your team down the field and lead them to victory, that's what a great player is to me."

— Jimbo Fisher

over the middle for the game-winner with just 13 seconds to go.

"It's the best football game he played all year, and I'll tell you why," Fisher said. "Because for three quarters he was up and down, and he fought. And just like any great player, some nights you don't have it.

"When you can come back like the great ones do, it's not my night, but we've got a chance to win this ballgame. It's the fourth quarter, I've got one or two touches left and you can take your team down the field and lead them to victory, that's what a great player is to me."

Winston was far from great early, completing just 11-of-24 passes for 120 yards in the first three quarters. But he finished by going 9-of-11 for 107 yards in the fourth quarter, including an 11-yard touchdown run to Chad Abram with 10:55 to go and the final touchdown to Benjamin.

The Heisman Trophy winner became the 14th player to win college football's most prestigious award and also claim a national title in the same season. FSU's Charlie Ward (1993) was among the group to do both.

FSU won its third national title exactly 20 years after its first and became the fourth team in the BCS

Rashad Greene races downfield for FSU. Greene led all FSU receivers with nine catches for 147 yards.

era to finish the season 14–0. It was the last national title game of the BCS, and it was arguably one of the best, on par with the Vince Young-led Texas win over USC in the 2006 Rose Bowl.

And three Seminoles will have their names among the best in a single season as they crossed the 1,000-yard plateau.

Running back Devonta Freeman had 73 rushing yards to give him 1,016 in his junior season. He is Florida State's first 1,000-yard rusher since Warrick Dunn in 1996. Freeman is just the eighth 1,000-yard rusher in school history.

Rashad Greene and Kelvin Benjamin became the first duo to have 1,000 receiving yards in a season since E.G. Green and Andre Cooper in 1995. Greene finished with 1,128 yards and Benjamin had 1,011 yards.

FSU also secured the FBS scoring record, putting up 723 points to snap the previous record held by Oklahoma in 2008 (716).

While the defense allowed Tre Mason to run for 195 yards, FSU also made the adjustments in the second half. The Seminoles kept Auburn off the scoreboard in the third quarter before allowing a touchdown and a field goal in the fourth quarter.

But in many ways, it was Winston who won it by again playing like a senior in the final minutes.

Winston grew up just a half hour from Alabama's campus and two hours from Auburn's campus. He considered both, along with Stanford and LSU, before choosing FSU in February 2012.

Now Winston and FSU have snapped the Southeastern Conference's seven-year winning streak in the BCS championship game. FSU won the first BCS title in 1999, and now it has the last one in 2013.

"I'm pretty sure people back home are going to say five championships in the state of Alabama because of me being from Alabama," Winston said. "Alabama people are going to try to keep it in their state however they can, but Florida State has the national championship." ■

Rashad Greene scurries through the Auburn defense after a key fourth-quarter catch. Greene's 49-yard reception on the game's final drive set up the game-winning score.

Kermit Whitfield breaks free and races down the sideline en route to his 100-yard kickoff return for a touchdown late in the fourth quarter. Whitfield's touchdown gave Florida State its first lead since early in the first quarter.

NATIONAL
CHAMPIONS

FLORIDA STATE. SEMINOLES. 2013

WINSTON'S STORYBOOK MOMENT

HEISMAN WINNER SHRUGS OFF SLOW START TO TAKE OFFENSIVE MVP HONORS

It was the worst possible time for Jameis Winston to have his first freshman moment. Cool and unflappable through Florida State's 2013 campaign, the reigning Heisman Trophy winner spent the first half of the BCS National Championship Game at the Rose Bowl looking like a first-year player straining under the weight of college football's biggest stage.

But in a game loaded with drama, Winston found his best when the spotlight shined brightest.

With his Seminoles trailing No. 2 Auburn by four points and 1:19 on the clock, Winston completed 6-of-7 passes for 77 yards and a 2-yard touchdown to Kelvin Benjamin that lifted FSU to a 34–31 victory and its first national title since 1999.

The Bessemer, Alabama, native, who celebrated his 20th birthday on Jan. 6, completed 20-of-35 passes for 237 yards and two touchdowns and was named the game's offensive Most Valuable Player.

"That's a storybook moment right there," Winston said. "I'm just so excited for our guys, man…and all I can say now is that we're champions. That's what matters to me."

For the game's first 30 minutes, Florida State looked like a much different team than the one that had romped through its schedule and Winston looked like a much different quarterback.

His throws missed the mark—sometimes close and sometimes by a wide margin. He was initially reluctant to throw the ball, often opting to tuck and run as open receivers ran downfield.

And Winston found himself constantly harassed by an Auburn pass rush that sacked him four times.

Winston went into the half having completed just 6 of his 15 passes and fumbled away a ball that Auburn parlayed into a touchdown that extended its lead to 21–3.

"[Auburn's defense] kept things mixed up," FSU coach Jimbo Fisher said. "I think they got pressure on him. They covered tightly, and we dropped some balls."

As the game shifted into the third and four quarters, though, Winston slowly began to find his rhythm. Fisher called several short and intermediate routes, allowing Winston and his

Jameis Winston proudly cradles the Coaches' Trophy after the BCS National Championship Game. The redshirt freshman quarterback was named the game's offensive Most Valuable Player after leading Florida State's game-winning drive.

receiving corps to get in sync.

He struck for his first touchdown pass early in the fourth quarter, an 11-yarder to fullback Chad Abram that essentially completed FSU's comeback from an 18-point deficit and cut Auburn's lead to 21–10.

Then, after a wild final five minutes in which FSU took a fourth-quarter lead then surrendered it on Auburn's subsequent drive, Winston stepped into the huddle at his 20 yard line with the national championship hanging in the balance.

"He was calm," junior receiver Rashad Greene said. "And he knew it wasn't over yet."

Winston would have his say before the end. He first hit Greene for a quick 8-yard completion that stopped the clock when Greene went out of bounds.

Then he hooked up with Greene again on a similar play, but this time Greene made his defender miss and took off, 49 yards down the sideline to put Auburn on its heels.

Four plays later, after Auburn's Chris Davis was flagged for pass interference in the end zone, Winston found Benjamin running across the face of the end zone, a step in front of AU's defender. The throw and catch made it look easy. FSU reclaimed the lead, 34–31, and the 13 seconds left on the clock weren't enough for the Tigers to find any more magic.

"I was ready," Winston said. "I wanted to be in that situation because that's what great quarterbacks do. That's what the Tom Bradys, Peyton Mannings, Drew Brees, that's what they do. Any quarterback can go out there and perform when they're up 50–0 in the second quarter." ∎

Jameis Winston looks for an open receiver against Auburn. Winston completed 20-of-35 passes for 237 yards and two touchdowns, including the game-winning pass to Kelvin Benjamin.

HEAD COACH

JIMBO FISHER

FISHER RETURNS FSU PROGRAM TO GLORY

There were plenty of times in the 2010 season when Jimbo Fisher's frustration was visible. The steam was building inside over the struggles of reshaping Florida State's football program.

In November 2010 FSU's promising 6–1 start began to turn very ugly. There were back-to-back losses: first at North Carolina State 28–24 on a goal-line fumble in the final minute and then 37–35 at home against North Carolina, which threw for 439 yards (and FSU also missed two field goals in the fourth quarter).

FSU was 6–3 and slipping back to its late 2000s form. In his first year after taking over for Bobby Bowden, Fisher then let loose a geyser of emotions at his Monday press conference following the loss to the Tar Heels.

"This team has to learn to develop a killer instinct," Fisher said in a raised voice during a lengthy rant, "and not hope to win but understand how to win. There's nobody on this football team that has. There's nobody on this football team that has reached that level and understands what it takes."

Fisher was calling out his players. FSU in 2010 was loaded with players that had never even won an ACC title, something the Seminoles had accomplished on an almost annual basis in the 1990s. He was challenging them to prepare and practice harder, to play smarter.

The wins and losses from 2010 reminded that the rebuilding job wouldn't be achieved in a season. Fisher knew that it would take time and he often referenced "the process." And that it would take the right mind-set by the players, which he emphasized as a need to change the culture from one that accepted a few losses here and there to one that couldn't stand losing.

Fast forward three years, and Fisher has led FSU to back-to-back ACC titles and now a national title. In four years he's built more than a championship team. It's what he thinks is a program that will be able to sustain success for the long haul.

"What I love about what we're doing right now—we're becoming a program," Fisher said. "I've always said that teams come and go. Programs sustain the test of time."

Jimbo Fisher, who began coaching at Florida State as an assistant in 2007, looks on.

The past few seasons, it was clear that Fisher and his staff were on the right track. And it was evident that the players were responding to the challenge.

Fisher and his staff recruited better, but it was more than just winning the services of five-stars and four-star players. It was finding the right athlete who was willing to not just bring his talent to Tallahassee, but also would be coachable and self-motivated. And it wasn't about making himself better, but also those in his position group and then the team.

The results began to show the progress, first on the recruiting trail as top players signed each February to play for FSU. But still every season there was a stumble or two. Even 2012, a season that saw an ACC title and an Orange Bowl win, ended 12–2. There was celebration but also disappointment, too. It was a not-so-subtle reminder that FSU was improving year-to-year but not yet achieving what it should as a program.

That's why fans took the 2012 losses so hard. FSU was supposed to have learned plenty from the losses.

This was a veteran team with a senior quarterback, playmakers, and pass rushers. But those losses at N.C. State and home against Florida were a reminder of what happens when you let your guard down and don't prepare well.

Remove 11 players that were drafted, including a trio of first-rounders in quarterback EJ Manuel, defensive end Bjoern Werner, and cornerback Xavier Rhodes. Remove seven starters on defense. Take away six assistant coaches.

Fisher made the right decisions this offseason, hiring defensive coordinator Jeremy Pruitt (a two-time national champion as an assistant at Alabama) and surrounding him with experienced assistants. He also brought in quarterbacks coach Randy Sanders, a former Tennessee assistant who had coached Peyton Manning in the mid-1990s.

Jimbo Fisher celebrates Florida State's 45–7 victory against Duke in the ACC Championship Game.

And Fisher chose redshirt freshman Jameis Winston in August, finally ending the summer-long drama over who would start at quarterback.

Through all the losses and the influx of new assistants, FSU made progress in 2013 and is 14–0. A regular season in which there were 13 wins and all but one of them a completely dominating performance.

"We had 11 guys drafted last year; 14 guys signed pro contracts," Fisher said. "We're able to come back with the senior leadership and some young guys that incorporate the program and our assistant coaches. And that's what we want. We want to be a program, not a team."

These Seminoles had to lose at first to understand how much more they needed to push each other and themselves to win. The players are having fun out on the field, of course, but what drives them more often than not is that they hate to lose.

The losses of 2010, 2011, and 2012 shaped the winning of 2013.

"We did envision this after last season because we left a lot out there on the table," senior linebacker Telvin Smith said. "We felt it was so much that we were supposed to accomplish."

What FSU has accomplished is building a program that aspires to do something special. Part of it was the chase for the national title. But the other aspect is restoring the program to where it once stood under Bowden in the 1990s and back to being a program that's one of the best—and in 2013 the No. 1 team—in the nation. ∎

Head coach Jimbo Fisher enjoys a laugh with his team, which rolled over its opponents by a cumulative 689–139 score during the regular season.

Florida State 41, Pittsburgh 13
September 2, 2013 · Pittsburgh, Pennsylvania

MONDAY NIGHT MADNESS

WINSTON NEARLY PERFECT IN COLLEGIATE DEBUT

By the time all the months of preseason hype and legend melted into Florida State's season-opening kickoff, it seemed virtually impossible that quarterback Jameis Winston could live up to the mountain of expectations that rested upon his shoulders.

In the end, though, defying conventional logic may have been the least of Winston's accomplishments in Florida State's season opener.

With a national audience watching and a sold-out Heinz Field setting the stage for Winston's collegiate debut, the redshirt freshman wasn't as good as advertised. He was better.

Winston completed 25 of 27 passes for 356 yards and accounted for five total touchdowns to lead No. 11 Florida State to an emphatic 41–13 victory over the Pittsburgh Panthers.

"I was so anxious. Everyone was excited," Winston said. "It's Monday Night Football. We're in college, playing on Monday Night Football in a pro stadium? I was so pumped for that."

The win is FSU's fourth in as many season openers under Jimbo Fisher. The Panthers, who made their Atlantic Coast Conference debut, started 0-1 for the second consecutive year under coach Paul Chryst.

The Panthers appeared ready to make things interesting with a first drive that went 80 yards in nine plays and ended with a 4-yard touchdown pass from Tom Savage to Manasseh Garner.

"Those guys came out and punched us in the mouth," senior defensive back Lamarcus Joyner said.

After FSU was forced to punt after its first possession, Pitt might've extended its lead on its subsequent drive, but true freshman Jalen Ramsey, who started at cornerback, picked off Savage and added a 31-yard return to the Panthers' 24-yard line.

Two plays later, Winston floated a pass down the seam to Nick O'Leary, who tied the game with a 24-yard TD reception.

O'Leary later added touchdowns of two and 10 yards, matching his 2012 touchdown total just one game into the season.

The victory against Pittsburgh served as a coming out party for Jameis Winston, who threw for 356 yards and four touchdowns during the win.

"Toward the end of the night when they told us the numbers, we were like 'Dang, [Winston] balled out.'" senior receiver Kenny Shaw said. "But I'm proud of him."

And as Winston made his mark on the box score, so too did his offensive teammates.

Junior receiver Rashad Greene led the way with eight catches 126 yards and a touchdown, sophomore Kelvin Benjamin added 73 yards on five receptions, and Shaw contributed 94 yards on just for catches.

The Seminoles' running game got in on the action, too, spreading 110 yards across 19 carries between juniors Devonta Freeman and James Wilder Jr.

"I know the reason I was having a good night was because the guys around me were having a better night than I was," Winston said. "I knew we were going to come out there and lay it out on the line."

Despite surrendering occasional chunks of yardage, especially early, FSU's defense limited the Panthers to 297 total yards (96 rushing) and intercepted Savage twice.

The Seminoles also sacked Savage three times— two of which came via edge rushes by cornerback Lamarcus Joyner.

"That was something coach emphasized this off-season," Joyner said. "He said I was too much of a good player not to come off the edge and try to make those kinds of plays, and that's what the defense is expecting me to do. It was successful."

After the game, Joyner of course fielded questions about FSU's defense. But the horde of reporters surrounding him couldn't help but steer their queries back to Winston.

Joyner said Winston first caught his eye as FSU's scout team quarterback in 2012, when the then-freshman would routinely make throws that Joyner, a four-year veteran, had only seem from the

Running back James Wilder Jr. rushes for some of his game-high 59 yards during the win.

"I know the reason I was having a good night was because the guys around me were having a better night than I was. I knew we were going to come out there and lay it out on the line."

— Jameis Winston

arms of first-round draft picks Christian Ponder and EJ Manuel. And, even then, only during their senior years.

So while Winston's debut may have taken the college football world by storm, his teammate was hardly surprised.

"I just call it a prophecy being fulfilled," Joyner said. "I knew since this guy's freshman year, (when Winston was) out there on scout team making plays a fifth-year senior, EJ Manuel was making, throws like that. And I just said to myself 'This guy is going to be special.'" ■

(Top) Ethan, Jimbo Fisher's son, who suffers from Fanconi anemia, hands his father a cupcake after the game. (Bottom) The Fishers pose with the Stevensons, a Pittsburgh-area family, who lost their son, Logan, to Fanconi anemia. During the game both Pitt and Florida wore helmet decals promoting the fight against the disease. (Opposite) Jameis Winston confers with coaches during his collegiate debut. The redshirt freshman completed 25 of 27 passes in Florida State's season-opening win over Pittsburgh.

Florida State 62, Nevada 7
September 14, 2013 · Tallahassee, Florida

WINSTON EARNS FIRST DOAK WIN

AFTER ROUGH START, FRESHMAN COMPLETES LAST 13 PASSES

The sequel to the Jameis Winston Show started slow.

After completing two of his first four passes, which already included as many incompletions as what he threw in the season-opening win at Pittsburgh, Winston overshot Kenny Shaw and was intercepted.

Florida State fans were on the edge of their seats, wondering what might happen next. There was drama, unexpectedly so, as the Seminoles were struggling at home against Nevada.

But then Winston completed his next 13 passes, connecting with Shaw and Rashad Greene on second-quarter touchdown passes as Florida State pulled away and routed Nevada 62–7 on Saturday afternoon.

"What I like about it was he made a mistake, but he didn't get gun shy," Florida State coach Jimbo Fisher said. "He went right back in and started making throws and made some good plays.

"They're going to happen in bigger games, in bigger moments. You just have to keep growing. You

have to remember he's just a freshman."

He had freshman-like moments early. But then he looked a lot like the Winston that was special in the opener—precise, poised and confident.

Winston threw for 214 yards and added a 10-yard touchdown run in the third quarter. And after starting his first game in Pittsburgh with 11 straight completions, Winston one-upped himself by finishing the game against Nevada with 13 straight completions.

Among those passes was a 24-yard touchdown pass, Winston's first at home, as he put just the right touch on the pass and found Shaw in the end zone after he had slipped behind a defender.

"It was a perfect throw in my opinion," Shaw said. "It just fell in my hands."

After throwing for 356 yards and four touchdowns in his first college game at Pittsburgh, Winston was more anxious to please—himself, his family, his teammates, and the 73,847 fans at Doak Campbell Stadium.

"First home game, I was just pumped," Winston

Though Jameis Winston threw his first interception of the season, he rebounded to lead FSU to a dominating 62–7 win.

said. "I tried to do too much. That's why I think I forced that turnover. I messed up."

It was the first college interception for Winston. And it came at a crucial point in the game, with Florida State ahead 3–0 but soon down 7–3 after Nevada capitalized with its first and only touchdown on Saturday.

Winston could have reacted the wrong way. But he was again composed in the face of adversity. And he received some words of encouragement from Fisher.

"He didn't give me no long speech," Winston said. "Didn't give me no long lecture. He just said, 'Go higher. Here it is. Adversity is here. What are you going to do?'"

Florida State had a three-and-out on its next drive. But then the Seminoles scored on nine of their next 10 drives as they scored 59 unanswered points.

Winston carved up Nevada in the second and third quarters, finishing the game 15-of-18 for 214 yards, three touchdowns, and the interception, and backup quarterbacks Jacob Coker and Sean Maguire played in the fourth quarter.

After the game, Winston was asked to evaluate his performance. And he again deflected praise.

"I never rate my performance because we got that victory," Winston said. "Victories, team. Losses, that's always the quarterback. I was just born like that."

The spotlight continued to shine brightly on Winston. And he handled the pressure well in his first starts. Despite the interception, it was a stunning opening two games: Winston was 40-of-45 (88.8 percent) for 570 yards, six passing touchdowns, and two rushing touchdowns.

Not bad at all for a junior or senior, let alone a redshirt freshman. ■

The Florida State band marches during the team's first home game of the 2013 season.

Florida State 54, Bethune Cookman 6
September 21, 2013 · Tallahassee, Florida

IMPERFECTLY DOMINANT

DESPITE DROPPED PASSES, FSU ROUTS FCS FOE

Wildcats coach Brian Jenkins called the Florida State–Bethune matchup a "heavyweight fight."

The battle of the bands was more worthy of top billing.

The matchup on the field, even in a year of FCS programs upsetting BCS powers, saw Bethune deliver a few jabs before Florida State threw the knockout punch.

In the end, it was a rout. Florida State ran for 266 yards and four touchdowns, and Jameis Winston threw for 148 yards and tossed two touchdown passes—overcoming at least five drops from his receivers—as the Seminoles ripped Bethune-Cookman 54–6.

And while Bethune is just an FCS team, FSU held the Wildcats under 10 points for just the second time in Jenkins' 39 games.

No. 8 FSU completed its third rout to open the season. The Seminoles, who kept the Wildcats off the scoreboard until the third quarter, outscored Pittsburgh, Nevada, and Bethune a combined 157–26 in the team's first three games.

Devonta Freeman ran for 112 yards on 10 carries, adding a 1-yard touchdown, as he surpassed the 100-yard mark for the second straight game. Converted safety Karlos Williams added 83 yards and two touchdowns, giving him three TDs in two games since moving over to offense.

"We did hit big plays," Florida State coach Jimbo Fisher said. "We ran the football well. Freeman, Karlos and (James) Wilder can hit the ball out of the park."

Winston completed 10 of 19 passes for 148 yards and two touchdowns. It was far from the accurate performances he had against Pitt and Nevada, and it was hampered by a high number of drops. But Winston also provided the game's biggest highlight in the second quarter.

The redshirt freshman dropped back, eluded two defenders, including one that had an arm on him, rolled left and, while falling down, found wide receiver Kelvin Benjamin for an 11-yard touchdown.

James Wilder Jr. was part of a running game that gashed Bethune-Cookman for 266 rushing yards.

"My first touchdown was going to be a negative in the film room," Winston said. "I was supposed to hot [read] the backside [receiver]. My mind was racing.... I wasn't even thinking about that hot.

"God blessed me with the talent, I shook him off. And then Kelvin was right there. Kelvin made a great play."

In his first three college games, Winston completed 50 of 64 passes (78.1 percent) for 718 yards, eight touchdowns and one interception.

Backup quarterback Jacob Coker entered the game on the second drive of the second half for FSU. Coker was 3 of 6 for 78 yards.

FSU's offense was sluggish early, fumbling deep in Bethune territory and dropping two would-be touchdown passes. Against Bethune, which routed Florida International 34–13 a week earlier, it didn't matter.

The Seminoles' defense was ready from the start. Bethune had a few first downs on its initial drive but linebacker Telvin Smith stepped in front of a Jackie Wilson pass and ran 68 yards for a touchdown.

FSU also added a safety early in the second quarter as Bethune (3–1) was called for holding with Wilson standing in the end zone and looking downfield.

The Seminoles played without two defensive starters, linebacker Christian Jones and defensive tackle Eddie Goldman, but kept Bethune off the scoreboard for the first 36 minutes of the game.

Filling in for Jones, Terrance Smith had 12 tackles through three quarters in his first college start.

"My whole goal was to make the best of the opportunity," said Smith, a sophomore. "It was very exciting to go out and compete and succeed."

Redshirt freshman Roberto Aguayo remained perfect on kicks. He had a career-long 45-yard field goal in the first quarter and made 7 of 7 extra-point attempts. Through three games, Aguayo made 5 of 5 field-goal attempts and 20 of 20 extra-point attempts. ■

Florida State saluted the armed forces during the Military Appreciation Day game against Bethune-Cookman.

25

MILITARY **DAY**
APPRECIATION

DA STATE UNIVERSITY

Florida State 48, Boston College 34
September 28, 2013 · Chestnut Hill, Massachusetts

SLOW STARTERS
SEMINOLES RALLY, OVERCOME 14-POINT DEFICIT

Florida State apparently needs to start slow only to wake up and pour it on.

The trend continued again Saturday. Before winning 48–34 the Seminoles trailed 17–3 at Boston College in the second quarter.

Florida State's defense put on a clinic—of how to not tackle. And Florida State's offense managed just a field goal and punted twice in the first quarter.

For the third time in four games, Florida State trailed early in the game. And this time the Seminoles were down 14 on the road.

But then everything changed. The defense forced BC to go three-and-out three times.

And Jameis Winston did what he has done all season—pick apart defenses with his arm and with his legs. He helped Florida State tie the game up at 17 and then saved his best play for the final one of the half.

With the ball on Florida State's 45, Winston took the snap from the shotgun, dropped back, dodged two would-be sackers, stepped to his right, and found Kenny Shaw, who went up over BC's Spenser Rositano and hauled in the pass in tight coverage, falling into the end zone for a touchdown.

Hail Mary. Shades of Doug Flutie, indeed.

"I just had confidence in Kenny," Winston said. "I have so many tremendous wide receivers to throw the ball to. I just knew we had score at the end of the first half."

Winston just keeps improving, understanding how to read defenses far better than many freshmen quarterbacks. And after a rocky start in which he completed just two of his first six passes, he rebounded with a 330-yard, four-touchdown game.

Just four games into his college career, Winston had already surpassed the 1,000-yard mark and had 12 touchdown passes. He had completed 73 percent of his passes and had just two interceptions in 91 passes.

The Heisman talk in September was incredibly premature. But Winston, as a four-game starter, had shown as much poise as a fourth-year senior.

"It's fun to watch him grow," Florida State coach Jimbo Fisher said. "He continues to grow and he makes plays…Big-time players make big-time plays."

And Winston spread the ball around, finding Kelvin Benjamin (three catches, 103 yards), Shaw (four catches, 93 yards, one touchdown), and Rashad Greene (four catches, 90 yards, two touchdowns).

Senior Terrence Brooks, who recorded a season-high seven tackles against Boston College, races down the field. (AP Images)

"He continues to grow and he makes plays... Big-time players make big-time plays."

— Jimbo Fisher

It was also the fourth straight game in which Florida State had 40 or more points.

Florida State adjusted well on defense, too. After BC put up 17 points early, the defense came through with three-and-outs on the next three drives.

For nearly 30 minutes, the Seminoles played some of their best defense of the season. They kept BC out of the end zone, allowing just a second-quarter field goal and a third-quarter field goal. And then…

Florida State also looked suspect on defense. BC showed Florida State that it can't fall asleep late in games. The Eagles drove 79 yards late in the third quarter and 75 yards early in the fourth quarter for late touchdowns.

The game was almost out of reach, but that second drive trimmed the Seminoles' lead to just 48–34 with 9:44 left. Those drives will frustrate defensive coordinator Jeremy Pruitt and fans alike. There were two interceptions, one of which was returned by P.J. Williams for a touchdown. But missed tackles in such a high quantity are also surprising.

It's not a sign of a top tier defense, which Florida State needed to be if it wanted to stay in the national championship picture.

"We have to clean up a lot of mistakes," Fisher said. "We have to get better. We have a long way to go." ■

Florida State defensive back P.J. Williams returns a fourth-quarter interception for a 20-yard touchdown. (AP Images)

Though his unit allowed three sacks on the day, Florida State offensive lineman Cameron Erving blocks Boston College linebacker Kevin Pierre-Louis during the first half of the 48–34 victory. (AP Images)

Florida State 63, Maryland 0
October 5, 2013 · Tallahassee, Florida

SENDING THE TERPS OUT IN STYLE

FSU SHUTS OUT MARYLAND IN TEAMS' LAST ACC MEETING

The showdown turned into a laugher. And while Jameis Winston and the offense deserve plenty of credit for putting up 63 points, just as important was the number Maryland had at the end of the day: 0.

Maryland was newly ranked at No. 25, an undefeated team with an offense that had averaged 39 points per game. The Terrapins were supposed to push Florida State, to see how good the Seminoles were, a litmus test with Clemson ahead on October 19.

Instead, Florida State pushed around Maryland. And it wasn't even close.

FSU's 63-point rout ties the largest margin of victory over a top 25 program in college football history. Shutouts are rare in football, especially over a top 25 program. Florida State now has its first shutout over a top 25 team since Georgia Tech in 1997.

"We played a couple of opponents that we should have shut out and we didn't get it done," FSU linebacker Terrance Smith said. "But to get the first goose egg feels good."

The Seminoles can enjoy this one and they can enjoy a bye week that focuses on Clemson and not

questions after being ripped by Boston College a week earlier. FSU gave up 34 points, still winning 48–34, but a performance like that leaves you open to questions.

Is this FSU defense as good as in previous years?

Was FSU really able to just plug in seven defensive starters and still keep on cruise control?

Is there something amiss with defensive coordinator Jeremy Pruitt's schemes? Or is there reason to panic or is this the normal growing pains of a defense that is still learning?

After a week of questions, FSU's defense answered the call.

Maryland couldn't run, managing just 33 yards on 25 carries. Terrapins quarterback C.J. Brown was knocked out of the game in the second quarter, and backup Caleb Rowe didn't manage to do much after Brown left the game. Star receiver Stefon Diggs was even held to just two catches.

"As good as we played on offense, we played better on defense," FSU coach Jimbo Fisher said. "[Maryland has] very explosive skill guys, and I thought our guys covered well, we rushed well, we

Quarterback Jameis Winston threw for 393 yards and five touchdowns during the statement victory against Maryland.

The Florida State fans recognize Bill Durham (second from right), the 1965 FSU graduate who came up with the tradition of a student portraying Osceola while riding a horse named Renegade and planting a flaming spear at midfield to begin every home game.

"As good as we played on offense, we played better on defense. Our guys covered well, we rushed well, we covered the quarterback. [The] defense played outstanding from start to finish."

— Jimbo Fisher

covered the quarterback. Defense played outstanding from start to finish."

Players said that the practice leading up to the Maryland game was crisp and focused. And the Seminoles delivered.

In the locker room before FSU took the field, defensive tackle Timmy Jernigan decided it was time for him to stand up and speak to the team.

"I really don't talk too much, but my message was just telling the guys that we haven't played a full game yet—offense, defense, and special teams," Jernigan said. "Expressing how much team means. There's not one guy out there. It takes all of us."

And it started with a defense that had been humbled by BC. FSU had given up 17 points early and then two touchdowns on long scoring drives in the second half.

FSU's defense responded, forcing Maryland to punt 11 times. The Terrapins had punted just 16 times in their first four games.

"We weren't very good; Florida State's a very good football team," Maryland coach Randy Edsall said. "If you can't run the ball, that makes it tough. They made us one-dimensional." ▪

Running back Devonta Freeman dives in a for a second-quarter touchdown from five yards out.

Florida State 51, Clemson 14
October 19, 2013 · Clemson, South Carolina

STATEMENT GAME
WINSTON, 'NOLES ANNIHILATE TIGERS IN DEATH VALLEY

Florida State earned a seat at the big-boy table. The Seminoles shredded Clemson's defense for 564 yards and frustrated Tigers quarterback Tajh Boyd into turnover after turnover.

The showdown between two of the nation's top five teams, just the fourth time it happened with two ACC teams facing off, was instead a one-sided knockout by the Seminoles.

Lamarcus Joyner forced two fumbles and had an interception in the first 12 minutes of the game, and Jameis Winston threw for a career-high 444 yards and three touchdown passes as the No. 5 Seminoles dominated No. 3 Clemson 51–14 on Saturday night before a sold-out crowd at Death Valley.

"The key tonight was defense," Florida State coach Jimbo Fisher said. "They were able to create them [turnovers], and then we were able to convert off them."

Winston increased his season total to 20 touchdown passes, solidifying his status as a Heisman Trophy contender. He completed 22-of-34 passes against Clemson to notch his fourth 300-yard game in just six career games.

Rashad Greene had eight catches for 146 yards and two touchdowns for Florida State, which scored at will on Clemson from the start. The Seminoles had a touchdown or field goal on eight of their 11 drives in the game.

"We don't play against noise. We're playing against the Clemson Tigers," Winston said. "It was amazing when we were out on the field that first snap. It was loud, and we started smiling because we don't play against noise."

Florida State's defense turned in its best performance of the season in what was a huge test against Boyd, a quarterback who had burned Florida State the previous two years. And Heisman voters voters likely crossed Boyd off their list.

Boyd's first pass was a completion to Stanton Seckinger, but he fumbled and led to Florida State's first touchdown. On Clemson's third drive, Boyd was sacked by Joyner, and the fumble was scooped up by Mario Edwards Jr, who ran 37 yards for a touchdown. And Boyd was intercepted on Clemson's final drive of the half, leading to a Florida State field goal.

It was one of the worst first-half lines of Boyd's distinguished career—11-of-24 for 99 yards and a

Wide receiver Rashad Greene, who had 146 receiving yards during the impressive victory, celebrates after scoring one of his two touchdowns on the day. (AP Images)

Wide receiver Kelvin Benjamin eludes Clemson cornerback Darius Robinson for a first-half touchdown. (AP Images)

"This was an opportunity for us to show them and we embraced that challenge."

— Lamarcus Joyner

touchdown. And his night didn't get much better as the Tigers went punt-interception-punt in the third quarter. Boyd finished 17-of-37 for 156 yards.

The Seminoles hadn't won at Death Valley since 2001, a five-game losing streak. But on this day, they owned the place. After Florida State went ahead 17–7 in the second quarter, you could hear a pin drop—and then just a war chant from a small contingent of Seminoles fans among the capacity crowd of 83,428 Clemson fans.

Florida State (6–0) had opened 5–0 three times in 11 seasons (2003, 2005, and 2012) but lost Game 6 each time. The Seminoles improved to 6–0 for the first time since they won their last national title in 1999.

The Seminoles are once again in the hunt.

There were plenty of doubts about the strength of Florida State's schedule in the first five games. A 63–0 rout of No. 25 Maryland said plenty. But the win over Clemson was a thrashing that clearly caught the attention of the nation.

Early in the fourth quarter, the majority of the Clemson faithful had left. Death Valley was silenced. That silence spoke volumes.

"We believed as an organization," Joyner said. "But the world knew? I doubt it. This was an opportunity for us to show them and we embraced that challenge." ■

Wide receiver Kelvin Benjamin, who had 62 of Florida State's 444 receiving yards on the day, makes an acrobatic grab during the first half. (AP Images)

A TRIO OF TARGETS

GREENE, SHAW, AND BENJAMIN IGNITE FLORIDA STATE OFFENSE

Despite all his playmaking theatrics, it would have been awfully difficult for Jameis Winston to win the Heisman Trophy without having a few capable receivers at his disposal.

In junior Rashad Greene, senior Kenny Shaw, and third-year sophomore Kelvin Benjamin, Winston and the No. 1 Florida State Seminoles might have the best receiver trio in the nation.

Each caught at least 50 passes. Each averages more than 70 receiving yards per game.

And each entered the BCS National Championship Game with a chance at a 1,000-yard season, which would make FSU just the fifth team in Football Bowl Subdivision history to have three receivers hit that mark.

"That's one thing about playing quarterback at Florida State," Winston said. "You have great guys that are going to get the ball…Those guys are amazing, Kenny, Rashad, 'KB', even [junior receiver] Christian Green, everyone has been playing their role with this team."

FSU hasn't had any receiver reach the 1,000-yard plateau since Anquan Boldin did it in 2002.

"It means a lot for our offense just to have three receivers that you can get the ball to at any time and can make any plays," said Greene, who leads the pack with 67 catches for 981 yards. "We have a lot of confidence going in because I feel like defenses have to be honest with us. You know, you can't just double one guy and focus on one guy when you have two more that can do the same thing."

Greene has set the pace, but Shaw and Benjamin haven't been very far behind. Through 13 games, Shaw had caught 52 balls for 929 yards and six touchdowns, and Benjamin had 50 receptions for 957 yards—good for a sterling 19.1 yards-per-catch average—and 14 scores.

It's made life tough for opposing defenses, which have on occasion been able to slow down one or maybe even two of FSU's receivers for a time. Containing all three, though, has been virtually impossible.

Also complicating matters is junior tight end Nick O'Leary, a Mackey Award finalist who has added 33 catches for 557 yards and seven touchdowns.

"They're very efficient, and we're getting the ball to them in great situations," FSU coach Jimbo Fisher said. "Jameis is doing it and reading it and delegating the ball as far as coverage goes…And [the receivers] do a great job of understanding where the holes [in the defense] are.

"They're not only really intelligent in general, but they're very football intelligent."

And each has been on the receiving end of several of Winston's Heisman-worthy highlights.

Of Greene's nine touchdown receptions, five went for 20 or more yards, including a 72-yard catch-and-run that helped to break open the Seminoles' 51–14 win at Clemson.

Shaw, perhaps the group's best route-runner, was on the receiving end of what may be the signature play of FSU's season, a 55-yard

A deep threat, Kelvin Benjamin averaged an impressive 19.1 yards per catch and scored 14 touchdowns during the 2013 regular season.

touchdown pass from Winston that sent FSU on its way to a 48–34 victory over Boston College after the Seminoles fell behind 17–3.

Benjamin, though, might have the market cornered on jaw-dropping moments.

The 6'5", 234-pounder has steadily improved this season to the point where defenses have at times found him virtually impossible to cover. His play has inspired a slew of nicknames, including "freak," "specimen," and even "Avatar"—after the high-flying creatures from the 2009 film of the same name.

"We don't have anybody that can line up and match up physically with Benjamin," Duke coach David Cutcliffe said prior to FSU's 45–7 win over the Blue Devils in the ACC Championship Game. "He's just a monster and with great skills."

Benjamin then proved Cutcliffe true to his word with a five-catch, 119-yard performance that included touchdowns of 54 and 14 yards.

It was the last of a remarkable, final-month tear for Benjamin in which he roughed up Syracuse, Idaho, Florida (which entered the game with the nation's No. 3 pass defense), and Duke for a combined 23 catches for 458 yards and nine touchdowns.

"I think he's got to a point where he really realizes he can play, and the pressure's not on," Fisher said. "So he has true confidence."

And that's good for Winston, who, while no doubt responsible for his receivers' gaudy numbers, is also plenty aware that he's benefitted from such a full stable of talented targets.

"It makes my job easy," Winston said. "If any quarterback in the country had wide receivers like that, they'd be happy. I mean, because those guys are top notch guys. Any one of them can go first round. They are amazing." ∎

Rashad Greene led all Florida State receivers with 981 receiving yards during the 2013 regular season.

Florida State 49, North Carolina State 17
October 26, 2013 · Tallahassee, Florida

GRUDGE MATCH
FSU AVENGES 2012 LOSS TO N.C. STATE

Timmy Jernigan grabbed a pen and walked up to the dry-erase board in Florida State's locker room. He wrote four numbers and sat down.

No motivational speeches. No talk of how to play with focus or intensity or to leave it all on the field. Nothing needed to be said.

Just four numbers and a dash: 17–16.

The score of North Carolina State's win over Florida State in 2012.

"And we just sat and looked at it," Jernigan said. "That's all that needed to be said."

For all of its success in 2013, Florida State needed to close the book on part of its past. The Seminoles were determined to send a message to N.C. State early—that there would be no chance for the Wolfpack to repeat history.

Jameis Winston threw for 292 yards and had three touchdowns, and Devonta Freeman had two rushing touchdowns as Florida State routed N.C. State 49–17 before 80,389 fans at Doak Campbell Stadium.

Florida State's first half was a dominating display, a throwback to the dynasty days on an afternoon in which the Seminoles honored legendary coach Bobby Bowden.

The Seminoles scored five touchdowns in the first quarter, tying a school record. Florida State also surpassed the 40-point mark for a seventh straight game, also tying a school record.

The Florida State defense forced three turnovers and didn't allow a point in the first half before taking the rest of the day off.

After what happened in Raleigh, North Carolina, the previous season, Florida State sent quite the message.

"It definitely felt good," Florida State safety Terrence Brooks said. "I was very hurt last year by that game. We definitely were not going to let that happen again. That was definitely unacceptable."

Winston has delivered in every game this season. He just narrowly missed out on his fifth 300-yard game, finishing 16-of-26 for 292 yards. And he now had 23 touchdown passes in seven games, matching EJ Manuel's touchdown total from 14 games in 2012.

Bowden was asked before the game if he saw similarities between Winston and some of Florida

Lamarcus Joyner (20), Telvin Smith (22), and Christian Jones (7) celebrate Smith's fumble recovery against N.C. State.

Senior defensive back Terrence Brooks breaks up a play intended for N.C. State wide receiver Jonathan Alston.

"It definitely felt good. I was very hurt last year by that game. We definitely were not going to let that happen again. That was definitely unacceptable."

— Terrence Brooks

State's elite quarterbacks, specifically 1993 Heisman Trophy winner Charlie Ward.

"I don't compare them," Bowden said. "They weren't alike. Charlie weighed 185, this guy weighs 225. Charlie was 6', this guy is 6'4". Now, what they do remind me of each other—their accomplishments. This guy is seriously good."

Bowden won a pair of national titles and finished in the top four of the Associated Press poll every season from 1987–2000. He won with top-flight quarterbacks and defenses that were stifling.

His dynasty teams of the 1990s look a lot like Jimbo Fisher's 2013 team.

Florida State was dominating in the first half. The second half doesn't look good, but playing second- and third-teamers against N.C. State helps the younger Seminoles gain experience.

And gave Florida State's starters some extra rest going into the Miami game.

"We're definitely going to be ready for them and we're going to prepare well," Brooks said. "I can't wait. It's going to be a big stage and that's what we all want." ■

Legendary coach Bobby Bowden made his first return to a Florida State football game for the N.C. State contest.

8
RUNNING BACK

DEVONTA FREEMAN
GUTTY MIAMI NATIVE ADDS BALANCE TO EXPLOSIVE OFFENSE

Before each Florida State football game, the Seminoles gather in the locker room and watch an inspirational video while a player speaks a few words to his teammates before they take the field.

With the Miami Hurricanes in town on November 2, it was naturally Devonta Freeman's turn.

"I was just telling them boys, 'I'm going to lay it all on the line for y'all. I'm going to fight for y'all,'" the Miami native said after Florida State's 41–14 throttling of the Hurricanes.

"And I love them."

With the speech delivered, Freeman went out and made good on his promise.

He ran for 78 yards and two touchdowns. He caught six passes for 98 yards and another touchdown.

And he laid one thunderous shoulder into the chest of a Hurricanes defender and then couldn't help but flash Miami's trademark "U" sign with his hands.

"It's not really for the U. It's for Miami," Freeman said. "That's where I'm from. It's just emotional."

Freeman had no trouble discussing his feelings for his hometown team during the week leading up the game. The fact that his hometown team didn't bother to recruit him felt like "a slap in the face." Each time he plays the Hurricanes, the chip on his shoulder can't help but grow.

From Freeman's first touch, a 10-yard reception, it was clear that the 5'9", 203-pound junior was running just a little bit faster and hitting just a little bit harder.

"He was crunk, man," fellow running back James Wilder said. "To be able to play your home team and make that happen, it's amazing. That's the best feeling. That's like you competing versus your brother."

Freeman is now 3–0 for his career against Miami and has tormented the Hurricanes each time. In three games, he's combined for 224 rushing yards and five touchdowns.

And he found a new way to contribute this year—through the passing game. While FSU quarterback Jameis Winston struggled to find an early rhythm, Freeman helped the Seminoles get on track. His 5-yard touchdown run capped a 13-play, 72-yard scoring drive to open the game, and his

In his third year of action, running back Devonta Freeman rushed for 943 yards and 13 touchdowns during the 2013 regular season.

48-yard catch-and-run midway through the second quarter extended FSU's lead to 21–7.

And with the Hurricanes' defense focused on slowing down the receiver trio of Rashad Greene, Kenny Shaw, and Kelvin Benjamin, Freeman often found himself all alone, awaiting an easy pass from Winston.

"Tonight they kind of left me free," Freeman said, "and Jameis went through all his reads and he had an extra guy, and that was me."

Freeman said he had more friends and family in attendance than he could count, including his mother Lorraine, who only this season has been able to make the trip from Miami to see her son play.

And he didn't forget his roots once the score went final. Freeman greeted several Hurricanes on their way off the field, chatted a bit with former Miami great Clinton Portis and shared a quiet moment with UM running back Duke Johnson, who sat on a stretcher outside the FSU locker room after injuring his ankle during the game.

"That little guy, what a warrior," FSU coach Jimbo Fisher said. "You talk about a Seminole Warrior. You talk about guy that's heart and soul… there's not an ounce of bad in his whole body, and he's a tremendous human being."

Freeman and his fellow backs, Wilder and junior Karlos Williams, spent much of this season running in the shadow of Winston, whose Heisman Trophy-winning campaign grabbed most of the headlines.

He finished the regular season with 943 rushing yards on 162 attempts (a 5.8 average) and 13 touchdowns.

"That's one of the things that makes us complete—that we are a balanced team," FSU coach Jimbo Fisher said. "We can throw and make plays, but we can run the football…Our numbers on the ground are good, and we're always going to have balance." ■

Devonta Freeman bursts through the line of scrimmage against Syracuse. He averaged 7.3 rushing yards during the 59–3 victory.

Florida State 41, Miami 14
November 2, 2013 · Tallahassee, Florida

SUNSHINE STATE SLAUGHTER

FREEMAN GETS REVENGE WIN AGAINST HOMETOWN TEAM

Devonta Freeman went to Miami Central High, just 15 miles north of the campus of the University of Miami.

He grew up a Miami Hurricane fan.

The Hurricanes coaching staff, the Randy Shannon regime, wasn't interested in Freeman.

The running back's first scholarship offer came from Florida State's Jimbo Fisher. He took it, even when Miami jumped in late and tried to get Freeman to stay home.

Against the Hurricanes, between the second and third touchdown that he had, Freeman caught a short pass and ran down the sideline, stiff-arming a Miami defender as he went for extra yards. And then he flashed a "U" to the Miami sideline.

Personal? You bet.

The 205-pound Freeman ran for two touchdowns and had a 48-yard catch-and-run, racking up 176 offensive yards, as Florida State defeated Miami 41–14 in a top 10 ACC showdown before a record crowd of 84,409 at Doak Campbell Stadium.

"I dreamed of always doing good in the big games," Freeman said. "I didn't know who it was going to be against. It so happened it was going to be against Miami."

The Seminoles defeated a pair of top 10 teams in 15 days, including the 51–14 rout of then-No. 3 Clemson on October 19—knocking the Hurricanes and Tigers off by a combined 64 points.

And perhaps they sent a message that they deserve to have a spot in the national championship game, though there was still plenty of football left over the next month. The Seminoles did it by dominating their intrastate rival on both sides of the ball, winning the fourth straight game in the series.

"I feel like we can play with anybody in the country," Florida State defensive tackle Timmy Jernigan said. "We're just trying to get to Pasadena by any means necessary."

The Seminoles' defense was stifling, holding Miami to just 275 yards and shutting out the Hurricanes in the second half. Florida State forced

Devonta Freeman, a Miami native, starred against his hometown school, which initially spurned him.

Miami quarterback Stephen Morris to toss two interceptions in the second half, and the Hurricanes managed just 95 offensive yards after halftime.

On a night when Jameis Winston was accurate but also tossed a pair of first-half interceptions, Freeman provided the punch in Florida State's offense. He had 78 yards on 23 carries and 98 yards on six receptions, including a few screen passes that Freeman turned into long gains.

Winston played possibly his worst half of football and he still led Florida State on three first-half scoring drives, helping the Seminoles to a 21–14 halftime lead.

Winston completed 21-of-29 passes for 325 yards and the touchdown to Freeman. (He was 9-of-15 in the first half and 12-of-14 in the second half.) It was the fifth time in eight games that the redshirt freshman surpassed the 300-yard mark.

Morris showed pinpoint accuracy early, delivering a pair of touchdown strikes to Allen Hurns in the first half. But then Morris had just 75 passing yards in the second half and was intercepted twice after trying to force long throws downfield.

Florida State dismantled its biggest two ACC rivals. After the game, Florida State coach Jimbo Fisher was asked if he would consider ranking the Seminoles No. 1 on his coaches' poll ballot.

He artfully dodged the question, sort of like Freeman evading Miami defenders.

"This is a very good football team," Fisher said. "I love our football team." ◼

James Wilder Jr., who scored two touchdowns against Miami, dives for the end zone.

Dressed in Florida State colors, Lee Corso, an FSU alum, picks the Seminoles to defeat Miami as ESPN's *College GameDay* visited campus for the game.

Florida State 59, Wake Forest 3
November 9, 2013 · Winston-Salem, North Carolina

CAPTURING DEMONS
FSU TOTALS SIX INTERCEPTIONS AS DEFENSE LEADS ROAD WIN

With their path to Pasadena clear, the Florida State Seminoles took another step toward the BCS National Championship game on November 9 in Winston-Salem.

FSU's defense turned seven Wake Forest turnovers into 38 points and quarterback Jameis Winston threw two touchdowns in two-plus quarters of work as the No. 2 Seminoles cruised to a 59–3 victory over the Demon Deacons at BB&T Field in Winston-Salem.

Florida State, 9–0 for the first time since its previous national title season in 1999, strengthened its inside track to a spot in the championship game after No. 3 Oregon's loss to No. 5 Stanford earlier in the week.

FSU coach Jimbo Fisher, though, downplayed any talk of future aspirations after the game.

"Continue to play well and prepare to play well," he said. "That's all that matters. Then you put your head down and you wake up and if you're there (at the title game), you're there. But you can't worry about the coulda, shoulda, wouldas. Forget all that stuff."

With the win, the Seminoles also clinched their second straight ACC Atlantic division title, their third in four seasons under coach Jimbo Fisher.

Making his first start in place of the injured Terrence Brooks (concussion), FSU freshman defensive back Nate Andrews picked off two passes in the first half and returned the first 56 yards for a touchdown that put the Seminoles up 28–0.

On the next play from scrimmage, Andrews knocked the ball loose from Wake Forest running back Josh Harris, and fellow freshman defensive back Jalen Ramsey scooped the ball and ran 23 yards for a score.

Fisher doesn't permit freshmen to speak with the media, but Andrews' veteran teammates had plenty of praise for him.

"He had a big game," senior linebacker Christian Jones said. "We prepare for situations where some guys go down and we have younger guys that are able to step up and step in spots if something happened. Nate Andrews capitalized on his opportunity."

Andrews, linebacker Terrance Smith, defensive end Mario Edwards Jr., Jones, and defensive back

Florida State linebacker Christian Jones hits Wake Forest quarterback Tanner Price in the first half to force a fumble. (AP Images)

"We were sharp, we just had the short fields. The defense was playing so well.... It was a hard game, offensively, to get into, but that's just the way it goes."

— Jimbo Fisher

Marquez White all intercepted passes for the Seminoles, whose six total interceptions matched a school record set in 1991. Wake quarterbacks Tanner Price and Tyler Cameron combined to complete 7 of 25 passes for 63 yards and three interceptions each.

"I'd like to say it was totally us shooting ourselves in the foot, but a big part of that was Florida State," Demon Deacons coach Jim Grobe said. "I give them a lot of credit. That's a good football team."

FSU's defensive dominance, though, came at the slight expense of its offensive statistics. Of the Seminoles' five touchdown drives, only two came from beyond 15 yards—the others came on the heels of turnovers.

Winston completed 17 of 28 passes (60.7 percent) for 159 yards, two TDs, and an interception. Florida State was held under 300 yards of total offense for the first time since the 2011 Champs Sports Bowl, a fact skewed by the fact that the Seminoles played with reserves for most of the second half.

Florida State defensive back Jalen Ramsey celebrates Nate Andrews' pick-six against Wake Forest by jumping into the arms of Andrews (29). (AP Images)

"We knew that our defense had their work cut out for them, but a lot of people overlooked Florida State's defense."

— Jim Grobe

Backup quarterback Jacob Coker entered the game early in the third quarter and finished 4 of 9 for 37 yards.

"We were sharp, we just had the short fields," Fisher said. "The defense was playing so well.... It was a hard game, offensively, to get into, but that's just the way it goes."

Wake Forest's only points, a 23-yard field goal early in the fourth quarter, were immediately answered by FSU freshman Levonte Whitfield, who returned the ensuing kickoff 97 yards for a touchdown. It was Florida State's first kickoff return for a touchdown since 2008.

The Demon Deacons managed just 165 yards of total offense, more than a third of which came via the legs of Harris. The senior carried 15 times for 65 yards, but also lost a fumble.

"We knew that our defense had their work cut out for them, but a lot of people overlooked Florida State's defense," Grobe said. "My biggest concern going into the game was not necessarily taking care of the football but getting first downs." ■

Florida State quarterback Jameis Winston, who threw for 159 yards before resting during much of the second half, scrambles to avoid Wake Forest's Nikita Whitlock in the first half. (AP Images)

Florida State 59, Syracuse 3
November 16, 2013 · Tallahassee, Florida

FOCUSING ON FOOTBALL

POISED WINSTON LEADS FSU IN ROUT AGAINST ORANGE

For three hours and 11 minutes, Jameis Winston was able to focus on football.

He was locked in, completing his first 11 passes.

He was accurate, finishing 19-of-21 for 277 yards and two touchdowns *by halftime*.

He ran 35 yards down the field, diving to block Syracuse defensive back Julian Whigham to spring Kermit Whitfield for a 74-yard touchdown.

Playing just days after he was linked to an alleged sexual assault from a December 2012 case, Winston was composed and confident as he led Florida State to a 59–3 win against Syracuse.

"Jameis played exceptionally well," FSU coach Jimbo Fisher said. "His mind was really in the game."

Florida State got the ball first, and when Winston's name was announced, the crowd of 74,491 at Doak Campbell Stadium cheered. Winston guided the Seminoles to a six-play, 77-yard drive that finished with a James Wilder Jr. 3-yard touchdown run.

The Seminoles had a touchdown on their first five possessions and added a field goal on the sixth. Rashad Greene caught a touchdown pass from Winston, giving FSU a 28–0 with 40 seconds left in the first quarter. By halftime, Florida State was ahead 38–0.

"When you have great veterans around you and you have people that you trust, you want to go out there on that battlefield and play your heart out," Winston said.

He did that on Saturday, turning in what was his most efficient effort since he completed 25-of-27 passes for 356 yards in a season-opening win at Pittsburgh. This wasn't a gaudy, stat-filled, 300-yard performance. If Fisher had wanted him to, Winston could have played a few more third-quarter drives to build up the stats. But that simply wasn't needed.

Winston showed the ability to block out the distractions of the previous few days and delivered drive after drive. He spread the ball around to his receivers and read the defense well.

Wide receiver Rashad Greene, who caught a six-yard touchdown pass in the first quarter, ascends for the ball.

The 1993 championship team, including coach Bobby Bowden, was recognized during the 59–3 victory against Syracuse.

"Once our offense gets in that groove, it's hard to slow us down."

— Jameis Winston

Florida State scored 40 points for the 10th straight game this season, extending the school record. The Seminoles also became the first team in the past 10 seasons to win three conference games by more than 55 points.

In addition to Winston's strong play in the passing game, Florida State rushed for 225 yards, a group effort, which was led by Karlos Williams' 78 yards on just four carries.

"Once our offense gets in that groove, it's hard to slow us down," Winston said.

Winston's day was done at halftime, and he smiled from the sideline as backup quarterback Sean Maguire threw a touchdown pass. And he ran out on to the field to celebrate with the defense after Chris Casher returned a fumble for a touchdown.

Florida State honored the 1993 team, celebrating the 20th anniversary of the Seminoles' first national championship. It wasn't lost on Winston what that 1993 team did and the parallels to what the 2013 team is trying to accomplish.

"We want to be elite. We want to be great," Winston said. "Just like when we had the '93 championship team, we want to be just like that those guys. We want to keep everything rolling." ■

Defensive tackle Timmy Jernigan brings down Syracuse running back Devante McFarlane for one of his six tackles in the victory.

DEFENSIVE COORDINATOR

JEREMY PRUITT

FORMER BAMA ASSISTANT MOLDS AGGRESSIVE, TURNOVER-FORCING D

Florida State's defense was expected to go through some growing pains after losing seven starters to the NFL, including a pair of first-round picks in defensive end Bjoern Werner and cornerback Xavier Rhodes.

Three of four defensive assistant coaches left for other jobs, including defensive coordinator Mark Stoops (who took over as Kentucky's head coach).

There were a few speed bumps early, especially during a 48–34 win at Boston College on September 28. The Seminoles allowed just 79 points in the nine games leading up to the BCS championship game.

Despite the turnover, Florida State's defense improved, and much of the credit goes to first-year coordinator Jeremy Pruitt. Coach Jimbo Fisher lured Pruitt, who won a pair of national titles as Alabama's defensive backs coach, to Tallahassee to replace Stoops.

And Pruitt delivered. Including his time at Alabama, Pruitt's combined record the past three years is an almost impossible to comprehend 39–2.

Pruitt was one of five finalists for the Broyles Award, presented annually to the nation's top college assistant coach. While he didn't win, it was a reward for how well Pruitt has done in his first year at FSU.

"I want to thank [Fisher] for going out on a limb and hiring a guy that's only been a college assistant for three years," Pruitt said at the Broyles Award banquet in December. "Think about that. I was defensive backs coach at Alabama, where everybody in the country knows who the DB coach is, and that's Nick Saban. I'm not ashamed to say it. He is the DB coach. Everybody knows it. All you have to do is run the film.

"For Coach Fisher to go out on limb to offer me a coordinator job, I owe him a lot. For him to believe in me and have faith, I'm truly thankful for that."

Fisher is clearly thankful for Pruitt, too. When Stoops left for Kentucky, Fisher set out to find a new defensive coordinator. And he put a priority on turnovers—and the aggression that forces them.

Starting in 2010, the Seminoles forced 27 turnovers (26th most in the nation), 23 (49th) in 2011, and 21 (66th) in 2012. Those numbers are

In his first year with Florida State, Jeremy Pruitt made all the right defensive calls.

hardly bad, but if there was one thing missing from those defenses, a consistent ability to get takeaways was it.

An inability to force a key turnover cost FSU dearly in one-point losses to Virginia in 2011 and North Carolina State in 2012.

Enter Pruitt.

Pruitt's pedigree as a defensive assistant at Alabama, where the Crimson Tide ranked No. 13 in turnover margin in 2012, suggested that changes would be coming.

And despite Pruitt's insistence that his approach to FSU's defense would be more evolution and less revolution, the Seminoles' players almost singularly revealed in the spring that this defense bore hardly any resemblance to what they were used to.

It was more aggressive, they said. It put the players in position to make big plays. It was fun.

Pruitt got FSU to buy into the need to force more turnovers. The Seminoles had 25 interceptions going into the BCS championship game, tops in the nation.

Just about everyone has had a part in the interception party, as 16 players have at least one. True freshman Nate Andrews had four interceptions, Telvin Smith had three, while Ronald Darby, P.J. Williams, Terrence Brooks, and Joyner had two apiece.

"Pruitt is amazing," Brooks said. "His defense is really good. Everyone is really buying into it."

The Seminoles have enjoyed one of their best defensive seasons in a decade. They lead the nation in scoring defense (10.7 points per game), the lowest total since FSU allowed just 10.2 points per game in 2000.

"He's had a great year," Fisher said of Pruitt.

"Our defense has had a great year. It's been a huge part of our success."

Pruitt has turned a very good Seminoles defense into an even better one in 2013 with more aggressive schemes. He loves to blitz, often sending cornerback Lamarcus Joyner after the quarterback and he likes to show multiple defensive fronts.

In the days after Pruitt was hired in January, Rhodes and Werner decided to leave FSU after their junior years. Joyner and linebacker Christian Jones debated their decisions, and in many ways, it was Pruitt who talked made the rising seniors comfortable with the new defensive schemes that he would be employing.

"Jimbo laid out what he wanted defensively," Pruitt said at the Broyles event. "This is what we want to be. This is what we've got; this is who we are. Our seniors were coming back. They grasped it and they took it and ran with it."

Convincing a few more seniors to stay was key in maintaining stability, even though both changed positions. Jones moved to rush end, and Joyner wanted to switch from safety to corner. And he was rewarded by being named a consensus All-American.

"I just remember having a conversation with Coach Pruitt over the phone, and from that conversation I knew what kind of character man he was," Joyner said. "To see him come in and to see his hunger to get this program better and install his defense and his philosophy around here, it was just a great experience.

"It was almost that love-at-first-sight thing, just meeting him and just speaking with him. Just the intelligence he has and the care and the love he has for the game and to make kids better around him, it was kind of easy for all the guys buy into it."

While the upperclassmen bought in, two true

freshmen defensive backs contributed more than was expected.

Andrews, initially thought to be facing a possible redshirt season, found playing time both as a fill-in starter and as a backup defensive back. He had 31 tackles. Another true freshman defensive back, Jalen Ramsey, has started every game while recording 44 tackles and an interception.

"They're going to be really good in the future," Brooks said, "probably better than we are, to tell the truth."

It signals a remarkable turnaround for an FSU defense that as recently as 2009, a year before Fisher took over as head coach, fielded a defense that ranked among the worst in school history—108th in total defense, 108th in rushing defense, 94th in scoring defense, and 77th in pass defense.

But as it turns out, that was only Phase 1. Now, with Pruitt, Florida State has the nation's No. 1 defense.

"In the past we were a great defense, a little more conservative," Joyner said. "Now we're being very aggressive." ■

Overseeing a defense that allowed just 10.7 points per game during the regular season, Jeremy Pruitt had a lot to

Florida State 80, Idaho 14

November 23, 2013 · Tallahassee, Florida

OFFENSIVE EXPLOSION

FSU SETS SCHOOL RECORD FOR POINTS IN FINAL GAME AT DOAK

Jameis Winston and an overpowering running game delivered Florida State's biggest offensive performance in school history.

Winston had four touchdown passes, Karlos Williams had two touchdowns, and both Telvin Smith and E.J. Levenberry had interception returns for a touchdown as FSU routed Idaho 80–14 at Doak Campbell Stadium.

FSU broke the school record of 77 points, which was set in 1995 in a 77–17 win against North Carolina State.

FSU also surpassed the 40-point mark for the 11th straight game, extending another school record. And the 2013 team has the record for most points in a season, with 607 points—and three games to go.

"I'm not disappointed at all, but I don't think we played our best," FSU coach Jimbo Fisher said.

While it's the most points that a Fisher-led team has ever scored, he did say that his Salem (West Virginia) team scored 82 points against Samford when he was a quarterback in the mid-1980s.

Quipped Winston: "I guess we have to step our game up a little bit."

It's hard to imagine FSU playing much better

this season. The Seminoles enjoyed a perfect run at home for the first time since 2000. FSU defeated Miami 41–14 in a top-10 showdown, and as it turned out that was the closest game in Tallahassee. The Seminoles won their seven home games by a combined 408–61.

On Saturday, Idaho earned a $950,000 payday—and took plenty of lumps.

Just about everyone had a big play or touchdown, helping the seniors enjoy their final home game. Former Glades Central standout Kelvin Benjamin had two touchdown receptions, Kenny Shaw had 107 receiving yards and two touchdowns, and Devonta Freeman had a rushing touchdown for the seventh straight game.

Winston again was composed from the start. While he was being investigated on an allegation of sexual assault from December 2012 that surfaced publicly November 13, Winston took the field with the offense to cheers from an announced crowd of 65,000.

He led FSU to touchdowns on six of his eight drives, leaving the game early in the third quarter after a 21-yard touchdown to Benjamin that put FSU

Jameis Winston threw four touchdown passes in limited playing time against Idaho.

ahead 49–7. Winston completed 14-of-25 passes for 225 yards and four touchdowns.

It was the third straight game that Winston and the first-team offense were able to relax for most—or all of—the second half. And while Winston is a contender for the Heisman Trophy, Fisher said it wouldn't be right to leave him in to pad his stats against Idaho.

"People know he played well," Fisher said. "He played exceptionally well and he's on a great team. To me, stats aren't the key for awards. It's how well you play, how you dominate your opponent, and what you do."

FSU was again dominant on defense, too. Smith and defensive tackle Jacobbi McDaniel, both seniors, had interceptions. Levenberry, a true freshman, had one. And so did Keelin Smith, a former Treasure Coast standout.

The Seminoles' first-team defense allowed just a touchdown late in the second quarter. FSU held Idaho to just 59 yards on 35 carries.

The game was another blowout, but it was a special finale for the 24 seniors, including long snapper Philip Doumar of Jupiter, Florida. FSU's underclassmen wanted to give the seniors a memorable finish at Doak, and they can say they set a school record in their final home game.

"We know where this program has come from," Telvin Smith said. "We've grown with the program, with the coaches. We know how to go about things. When I first got here, Coach Fisher said we didn't know how to win. We learned how to win." ■

Linebacker Telvin Smith returns a first-quarter interception 79 yards for the score.

Florida State 37, Florida 7
November 30, 2013 · Gainesville, Florida

'NOLES CHOMP MUSCHAMP'S GATORS

BENJAMIN RIPS FLORIDA FOR NINE CATCHES, 212 YARDS

During the 37–7 rout of rival Florida, Florida State was off to an uncharacteristically slow offensive start. The Seminoles managed just a field goal on their first three drives, with one ending on an underthrown Jameis Winston pass that was intercepted and the other with a three-and-out.

Winston gathered the offense for Florida State's fourth drive, which was set to begin after a punt pinned the Seminoles at their own 4-yard line. He challenged his teammates, motivating them to work together and put together a drive that would be the launching pad for a win.

"Before that drive, I got the team together," Winston said. "And I said, 'Listen, guys, this is going to define this game right here. If we can just shove it down their throats this drive, we will win this football game.' And they looked me in the eye and they said, 'I got you.'"

From there, Winston to Kelvin Benjamin was almost an unstoppable combination. The freshman

quarterback pushed Florida State down the field on a 12-play drive, which culminated in a 45-yard catch-and-run in which the 6'5", 235-pound Benjamin broke four tackles and ran into the end zone.

Florida State took a 10–0 lead on Benjamin's touchdown and never looked back. Winston and Benjamin connected a total of nine times for 212 yards and three touchdowns.

The Seminoles moved to just a win away from a spot in the BCS championship game.

"One thing we discussed after the game, it's not over yet," Winston said. "We don't care who we play. It's a faceless opponent. Just because we're playing Duke that doesn't mean we're going to let up, that doesn't mean we think less of them. They deserve it."

Florida State deserves it, too. The Seminoles dominated Florida from the middle of the second quarter on. They racked up 456 yards of offense and allowed Florida just 193 yards and a fourth-quarter touchdown.

Benjamin had 19 more yards on Saturday

Quarterback Jameis Winston threw for 327 yards and three touchdowns during Florida State's rout of rival Florida.

than the entire Florida offense. And it was the best receiving game ever by a Seminoles receiver against Florida.

"'KB' has some real advantages with his size and speed and athleticism," Florida State coach Jimbo Fisher said. "He can be a very, very special player. He's starting to really develop into that guy."

Benjamin, a redshirt sophomore, now has 12 receiving touchdowns. It ties him for the fourth most in school history.

And Benjamin's day helped add to Winston's already impressive numbers as he pursues a Heisman Trophy. Winston completed 19-of-31 passes for 327 yards, and all three of his touchdowns went to Benjamin.

Winston increased his season total to 35 passing touchdowns, the most in a single season by any Florida State quarterback. Chris Weinke had set the record with 33 in 2000, the season he won a Heisman Trophy as a senior.

"Jameis has had an outstanding year," Weinke said in a text to FOX Sports Florida in the fourth quarter. "Records are made to be broken, and his consistency and accuracy throughout the year have earned him the right to hold that record.

"He has been fun to watch, and I couldn't be more proud of him."

The Winston-to-Benjamin combination overshadowed another dominating performance by Florida State's defense. And the Seminoles found motivation from a Will Muschamp quote from 2012.

In 2012, Florida ran for 244 yards and averaged 5.2 yards per carry in a 37–26 win at Florida State.

After the game, Will Muschamp celebrated a "sexy" win. And he said that the Gators had better rushing games against better SEC defenses than what Florida had accomplished against Florida State.

More than a year later, Muschamp's comments came back to bite the Gators. FSU coaches printed

Bryan Stork (52) and his fellow linemen pose with a gator head after defeating the Florida Gators.

off a copy of that comment in February and posted it in every locker.

"We don't ever want to be disrespected. We don't ever want to show weaknesses," Florida State defensive back Terrence Brooks said. "We really took that to heart this week."

And Florida State tackled with plenty of heart. The Seminoles knew that they needed to stop the run, especially with third-string quarterback Skyler Mornhinweg in the game. Florida State held Florida to just 78 rushing yards, which included a 50-yard run by Trey Burton in the first half.

Take out that long run, and the Gators had 23 carries for just 28 yards.

Florida State also blitzed Mornhinweg, holding him to just 115 passing yards. He completed 20-of-25 passes but rarely had time to throw downfield. The Seminoles' defensive backs keyed in on keeping the short passes to just that, not allowing long runs after the catch.

Florida State kept Florida off the scoreboard until the Gators scored their lone touchdown on a 5-yard pass from Mornhinweg to Hunter Joyer with 13:39 left in the game.

It was the biggest Florida State win against Florida since the Seminoles won 52–17 in 1988.

Florida State now has its fourth perfect regular season, adding to what the 1979, 1996, and '99 teams have accomplished. But now the Seminoles move on to the postseason and they are aiming for the program's first national title since the 1999 season.

"The sky is the limit," Brooks said. "We are never satisfied. We still have a lot more to prove. We're not going to stop until we get it." ■

James Wilder Jr. rumbles through the Florida defense for a chunk of his game-high 63 yards.

ACC CHAMPIONSHIP GAME

Florida State 45, Duke 7
December 7, 2013 · Charlotte, North Carolina

ON TO THE BCS CHAMPIONSHIP GAME

FLORIDA STATE CRUSHES DUKE FOR ITS 2ND STRAIGHT ACC TITLE

It's been 13 years since Florida State last played for a national title.

The No. 1 Seminoles now have a spot in the BCS Championship Game, and they did it with (what else?) a performance that showed their dominance while thrashing yet another team.

Jameis Winston threw for 330 yards and three touchdowns, further cementing his Heisman Trophy candidacy, and Florida State's defense held Duke in check in a 45–7 victory in the ACC championship game.

The Seminoles became the first team to win back-to-back ACC titles since Virginia Tech (2007–08). Florida State has 14 ACC titles, tying Clemson for the most in league history.

"This championship means a lot to us," Florida State coach Jimbo Fisher said. "This is where we want to be every year, and we have to get here to keep achieving and going to BCS games."

Florida State is the only Football Bowl Subdivision team that finished the season undefeated after losses by both Ohio State and Northern Illinois.

The Seminoles last played for a national title in 2000, falling to Oklahoma in the Orange Bowl. Florida State capped a perfect season in 1999 with a national title and a Sugar Bowl win over Virginia Tech.

For a decade-long stretch in the 2000s, Florida State was far from the dominant Seminoles teams of the 1990s. After Bobby Bowden was pushed into retirement after the 2009 season, Fisher was promoted.

He emphasized changing the culture, from one that often accepted eight- or nine-win seasons as acceptable. He pushed for ACC titles and now has won a pair of them.

"This is what I imagined," Fisher said. "We always imagine more."

Winston completed 19-of-32 passes, including two touchdown passes to Kelvin Benjamin (one of them a 54-yard catch-and-run) and another touchdown pass to Kenny Shaw.

In his final game before the Heisman Trophy voting closes, Winston didn't deliver his best game. But he surpassed 300 yards for the seventh time and added a 17-yard touchdown run in the third quarter.

Running back Devonta Freeman, who led all rushers with 91 yards, breaks a tackle in the ACC Championship Game.

Fisher was asked if Winston is the best player in the nation, and he smiled.

"I'm going to say this," Fisher said. "If he isn't, it's a short roll call. I'll promise you that."

The Seminoles also ran for 239 yards on 43 carries, averaging 5.6 yards per carry. It was the 12th time in 13 games that Florida State surpassed the 40-point mark.

Duke (10-3) couldn't get much going on offense, turning it over three times and punting nine times. A Blue Devils offense that has averaged 33 points per game this season was kept off the scoreboard for nearly 59 minutes until Josh Snead scored on a 5-yard run for Duke with 1:01 left.

Florida State has ripped teams by a cumulative 689–139. All of the wins have been by double figures, and it's notable that kicker Roberto Aguayo outscored teams by himself, 147–139.

The Seminoles went unbeaten despite a number of offseason obstacles. Florida State lost seven defensive starters to the NFL, not to mention a first-round pick in quarterback EJ Manuel. And Fisher had to replace six assistant coaches.

Seniors like Lamarcus Joyner and Christian Jones returned to the defense. The years of top 10 recruiting classes paid off, and Florida State filled the holes on offense and defense.

But Florida State was able to win week after week.

"We lost 11 players last year that got drafted," Fisher said. "To me that's a testament to our assistant coaches, how they got these guys ready to play. And how the senior leadership of the team developed a culture and a program that develops consistency."

Players said they felt in the spring that this team could take a step forward, even improving on Florida State's 12–2 record of a year earlier. That team won an ACC title and an Orange Bowl.

Senior Bryan Stork holds the Bank of America Stadium turf to be placed in a sod cemetery, a tradition that takes place after Florida State wins road games.

Devonta Freeman carries the ball against Duke. The FSU running back totaled 91 yards on 18 carries.

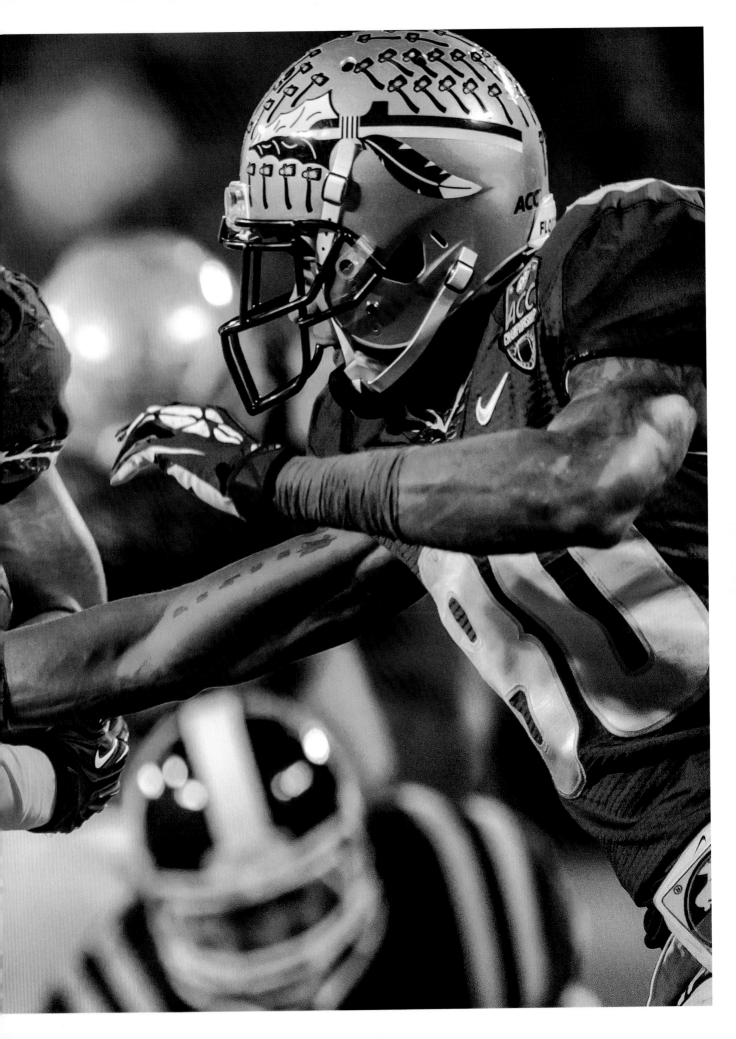

"We lost 11 players last year that got drafted. To me that's a testament to our assistant coaches, how they got these guys ready to play. And how the senior leadership of the team developed a culture and a program that develops consistency."

— Jimbo Fisher

But there was a feeling that, despite all the departures, Florida State could accomplish more.

"We did envision this after last season because we felt like we left a lot out there on the table," senior linebacker Telvin Smith said. "We felt like it was so much that we were supposed to accomplish that we came back and we had a little—not a vendetta—like coach said, it was a reckoning." ▪

Lineman Bobby Hart (51) douses head coach Jimbo Fisher with Gatorade after the ACC Championship Game victory.

5
QUARTERBACK

JAMEIS WINSTON

REDSHIRT FROSH BECOMES YOUNGEST HEISMAN TROPHY WINNER IN NCAA HISTORY

Charlie Ward and Chris Weinke have company.

Jameis Winston, Florida State's redshirt freshman quarterback, wrote his name in both school and college football history on December 14 by winning the 79th Heisman Trophy at a presentation at the Best Buy Theater in New York.

The youngest Heisman winner at 19 years, 342 days, Winston breezed past a field of finalists that included the previous year's winner, Texas A&M QB Johnny Manziel, as well as Alabama's AJ McCarron, Auburn's Tre Mason, Boston College's Andre Williams, and Northern Illinois' Jordan Lynch.

He joins Ward (1993) and Weinke (2000) to form a trio of Heisman winners from Florida State, which lays claim to both the oldest and youngest players to win the Trophy.

"It's a blessing. I don't even know what's going on right now," Winston said while fighting back tears. "Honestly, I'm so happy. I'm so overwhelmed by this whole thing. This is the first time I've been speechless in a long time."

A former five-star quarterback prospect from Bessemer, Alabama, Winston entered his first season as a starter under a mountain of hype. But he answered the hype—and effectively launched his Heisman candidacy—with a star turn in his debut at Pittsburgh.

There, Winston completed his first 11 passes on the way to a 25-of-27, five-touchdown (four passing, one rushing) performance.

After the game FSU coach Jimbo Fisher cautioned against overreacting, warning that it was only one game and that Winston still had a long way to go.

But as the Winston-led Seminoles piled up win after dominating win, it was clear that he was no flash in the pan.

By the time the Seminoles wrapped up their second consecutive ACC championship, Winston had shattered records at the school, conference, and national level.

After becoming Florida State's third Heisman Trophy winner, Jameis Winston poses with the famous award. (AP Images)

THE HEISMAN MEMORIAL TROPHY
PRESENTED BY
THE HEISMAN TROPHY TRUST
TO
JAMEIS WINSTON
UNIVERSITY

His 38 touchdown passes are the most in FSU and ACC history and are the most by a freshman in Football Bowl Subdivision (FBS) history.

Winston's 190.1 passer rating is the best in the country, and he ranks in the top 10 nationally in completion percentage, touchdown passes, passing yards, passing yards per game, yards per completion, points responsible for, and points per game.

"He's the real deal," Ward said.

He's also the first freshman to quarterback his team to 14 wins after leading the top-ranked Seminoles to victory in the BCS National Championship Game.

Winston's season, though, isn't just measured in his numbers, but also by how he accumulated those numbers.

The 6'4", 228-pound, dual-threat quarterback dazzled with his ability to evade defenders, escape the pocket and, more often than not, find an open receiver for a highlight-reel play.

He did it against Bethune-Cookman, turning a twisting, defender-splitting scramble into a falling-down touchdown pass to receiver Kelvin Benjamin. And again a few weeks later when he threw a Maryland defender off his back, scrambled to his right, and found tight end Nick O'Leary in the back corner of the end zone for a leaping touchdown.

But the best of Winston's best might have come at the end of the second quarter in Chestnut Hill, Massachusetts. It was there against Boston College that the Seminoles faced the biggest threat to their undefeated season.

FSU started slow and fell behind 17–3 before Winston brought the Seminoles back, first with a 56-yard touchdown strike to receiver Rashad Greene and later with a 10-yard scoring strike to fullback Chad Abram. With the clock running down on the half, Winston made the play that will

The youngest Heisman Trophy winner in the award's history, Jameis Winston strikes the award's signature pose. (AP Images)

be shown on his highlight reel for years to come.

Winston received a shotgun snap with one second remaining and was immediately besieged by Eagles defenders. He slipped out of the reach of one, threw off another, and stepped into a deep throw—right as a third defender collided into his chest—that hit receiver Kenny Shaw in stride for a 56-yard touchdown that propelled the Seminoles to a 48–34 victory, their closest of the season.

"It couldn't have been more on the money," Shaw said. "I knew he could get it there. He can throw it probably on his knees to the end zone."

Winston played the final quarter of the regular season under the shadow of a sexual assault investigation that was made public despite the fact that he'd been neither arrested nor charged with a crime.

He played three games while the Florida state attorney's office conducted its investigation and appeared completely unaffected by any off-field issues, leading the Seminoles to blowout wins over Syracuse, Idaho, and arch-rival Florida.

Two days before the ACC Championship Game against Duke, state attorney Willie Meggs announced that Winston would not face charges and that the case was closed. The Seminoles went on to rout the Blue Devils 45–7 and clinch their first-ever 13–0 record and a chance to win FSU's third national title.

The investigation didn't cost Winston the Heisman, but it did lead 115 voters to leave him off their ballots entirely, meaning he could've won by an even larger margin.

"Just to know what he went through to get up there on that stage, sometimes as a coach it just hits you," Fisher said. "To me that's why you're in coaching: to watch them grow and achieve the things you know they're capable of when there are odds against them."

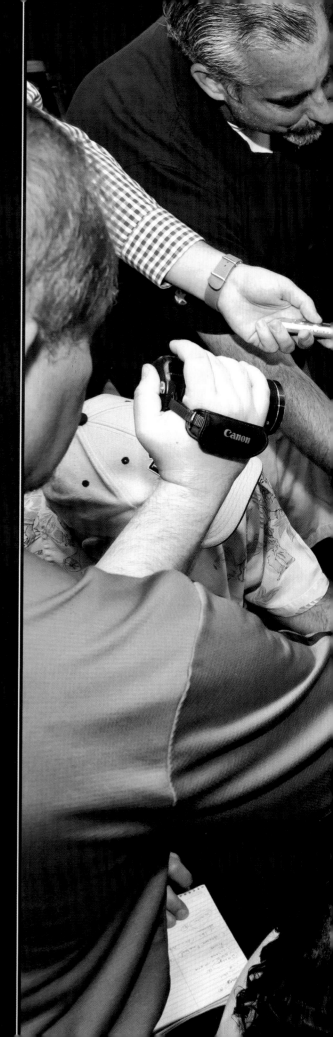

Always photogenic and sporting a grin, quarterback Jameis Winston meets with the media.

When Winston and his fellow finalists descended upon Times Square, the only remaining suspense surrounded Winston's margin of victory and who would finish second.

That turned out to be Alabama's McCarron, who had 79 first-place votes. Lynch finished third, followed by Williams, Manziel, and Mason.

As has often been the case since Labor Day, this night belonged to Winston, who traded in his garnet and gold uniform for a black suit with peak lapels, white shirt, and black-and-blue plaid tie.

After Heisman trustee Jim Corcoran called his name, he flashed his trademark grin and made his way on stage where he lifted his 25-pound trophy.

He gave a short, emotional speech in which he repeatedly spoke of "trusting in the process"—a mantra of Fisher's.

He used the phrase to describe his days as a youngster in Bessemer and also his decision— aided by FSU's baseball coaching staff—to say no to pro baseball and become a two-sport athlete in Tallahassee.

And Winston said he trusted the process again over the past month, when his name made headlines for reasons other than football.

"I trust in the process that evaluates facts, and its truth is delivered with positive outcomes," he said.

As Winston spoke, cameras cut to his parents, Antonor and Loretta, and to Fisher, who smiled while wiping tears from his eyes. He made reference to them; his high school coach; FSU baseball's Mike Martin and Mike Martin Jr.; and former FSU assistant Dameyune Craig, who now coaches at Auburn.

"This Heisman isn't just for Jameis Winston. It's for Florida State," Winston said. "I love everybody in here. I'm so blessed right now. It means so much to me." ∎

Jameis Winston, who completed 19 of his 31 passes against Florida, readies to throw.